Dragons, Slime and Soggy

Cool poems to inspire positivity, laughter and discussion.
With..... 'Discussion and Discovery Ideas' for parents, carers and teachers.
Includes 'Did you know?' boxes.

A.F. B. Griffey.... Illustrations....R. W. B.

Louannvee Publishing

Copyright © A. F. B. Griffey 2018
I See a Star copyright © R. W. B. 2018
Illustrations copyright © R. W. B. 2018

Moral rights asserted.

All rights reserved. No part of this publication may be reproduced, stored in a retrieval system, or transmitted, in any form or by any means electronic, mechanical, photocopying, recording or otherwise, without the prior written permission of the publisher.

Disclaimer

Whilst every effort has been made to ensure that the information, general knowledge and advice offered within in this book was correct at press time, the author and publisher do not assume and hereby disclaim any liability, to any person or persons, for any loss, damage or disruption caused by inaccuracies or omissions, whether such inaccuracies or omissions result from negligence, accident or any other origin.

'Did you know?' boxes – were taken from original teaching plans written by the author and used within the author's nursery and primary (Elementary) work-shops.

Discussion and Discovery Ideas for Parents, Carers and Teachers – were based on the author's experience and understanding re: discussion with 4 – 10's.

Parents, carers and teachers are responsible for the overall well-being of the children in their care and for deciding how to use, dismiss, simplify or extend information, general knowledge and advice, discovered within this book, to meet the needs and interests of children in their care.

ISBN   978-0-9935564-4-9

Published in the UK by:

Louannvee Publishing

www.louannveepublishing.co.uk

To parents, carers and teachers everywhere and to a fantastic granddaughter Ai Daisy.

This Book Belongs to:

_____

_____

Contents	Page
If I had a Dragon	5
The School Inspector and the Giant African Millipede	6 - 7
Back to School Tomorrow	8 - 9
Hooray for Ginger Hair and Freckles	10
I See a Bright, Bright Star	11
Our Grandma Lives on a Star	11
Slime Crime	12 - 14
Dragon Wishes	15
Dragons Were Here	16 - 17
Awesome Storm	18
Mum's Car Alarm Won't Stop its Whine	19
Verity the Venomous Viper	20 - 21
Itchy, Twitchy Fleas	22
Uncle's New Beard	23
Soggy Socks	24
Text	25
Big Brother's Chewing Gum Surprise	25
There's a Lazy Lizard in my Bedroom, Lying on my Bed	26 - 27
Discussion and Discovery Ideas for Parents, Carers and Teachers	28 - 31
The Author….The Illustrator	32

If I had a Dragon.....

I wonder what would happen
if I had a dragon as a pet.
Would he shake my hand, with his paw
and smile as soon as we met?

Would he eat toast, or meaty roast
and lie down on my bed?
Would he talk to me and read a book
and could I call him Fred?

Would he live in our house, as quiet as a mouse
and never breath fire indoors?
Would he clean his teeth and tidy up
and always wipe his paws?

OR..........

Would he swoop in with a crash and land with a splash
in mum's bubble bath full of bubbles?
Would he untidy my toys and make a noise
and then blame ME for all these troubles?

> **Did you know?** There is a tree called a **Dragon's Blood Tree**. Its **sticky liquid (resin)** is red in colour and can be used as a wood varnish.

The School Inspector and the Giant African Millipede

In our classroom is a mini beast tank,
complete with leaves and a mossy bank.
One day, whilst cleaning that mini beast land,
a millipede crawled onto my hand.

It was not a tiny millipede. It was a..........

Giant African Millipede!

Suddenly... out in the corridor we heard the sound,
of footsteps stomping along the ground.
They stopped at our door and we heard a knock.
Wow! A School Inspector. What a shock!

He looked at us with a long, cold stare.
I showed him the millipede. It gave him a scare.
He shivered. He shook. He couldn't keep still.
He truly looked most horribly ill......

Then..... **he shouted**.....

"There's a creature moving on your skin.
It's long. It's brown. It's very thin.
It's wriggling and squirming right up your arm.
I'm really afraid it will do you some harm.

"I can't stay now, but I'll come back again.
I don't know how and I'm not sure when."
He slammed the door and he started to run,
right out of our school and into the sun!

Our new School Inspector says
    Giant African Millipedes are really cute!

Did you know? Giant African Millipedes move quite slowly. When they are scared they curl into a tight ball. They can grow up to 38.1 centimetres (15 inches) long.

Back to School Tomorrow

Mum says it's school tomorrow;
the start of a new school year.
I feel a cool excitement
and….
a tiny bit of fear.

New classroom and new teacher;
Miss Barbara is her name.
New lessons and hard work,
but….
my friends will be the same.

So…..

I'm looking forward to school tomorrow,
being with my friends all day,
because....
in between the hard work,
there will still be time to play.

Did you know? Some children do not go to school. Instead, they study, discover and learn at home; taught by a parent, carer or tutor. They may join with other children and families to study and play together or to visit museums, galleries and other places of interest.

Hooray for Ginger Hair and Freckles

I have ginger hair and freckles.
I know I'm really cool,
but some kids like to tease me
on my way to school.

They call me nasty names
and laugh at me as well
and when they're being really horrid,
they tell me that I smell,

but......

They're just great big bullies.
I don't answer when they speak.
I know my ginger hair and freckles
make me quite unique.

So.....

Hooray for ginger hair and freckles.
I know I'm really cool.
I turn my back on bullies
and walk proudly into school.

I See a Bright, Bright Star

I see a bright, bright star, far, far away.

What its name is, I cannot say,   **but.....**

it's looking at me, from millions of years ago

and.....

its message of a twinkle just arrived to say hello.

> Written by our illustrator R. W. B.

Our Grandma Lives on a Star

Our Grandma's gone to heaven.
She lives on a star.
We can't go to see her.
We can't go by car.

Our Grandma's gone to heaven.
Heaven is too far,
but we know she loves us
way beyond each star.

> Thank you D (age 5) and your Mum, for sharing your thoughts and for letting me build them into a poem to share with others.

Slime Crime!

I really miss my giant pot of sticky, gooey slime, because....

Mum took it away when it made a mess
all over Aunties favourite dress.
I just squeezed the pot to raise the lid,
green slime slurped out and then it slid....
on Auntie's lap – upon her knee,
ran down her leg and I could see:
slime in her slippers.... yes.... right inside.
Then Mum shouted and Auntie cried.

So.....

I scooped the slime back in the pot.
Not all of it, but quite a lot.

I ran to the garden, to play with it there.
I was in trouble, but I didn't care.
I swung on the swing, swinging high,
with a view of trees and the blue, blue sky
and a slime ball squelching in one hand,
ready to throw…where would it land?

It shot up high – right over the edge,
of our broken fence and next door's hedge.

Wow…..

Mum's friend next door was lying flat,
sunbathing on a towel. Then.....Suddenly...... **splat!**
Her face was a mass of green, green goo.
All squishy and squidgy and sticky like glue.
She stood. She yelled "This is a crime,
my face is dripping horrid slime."

So.....

I said... "Just scoop the slime back in the pot.
Not all of it, but quite a lot."
I gave her a spoon and some tissue as well,
but she wasn't happy, I could tell.
Then when she had finished she put on the lid.
I said I was sorry....well....I think I did.
She gave the slime back and I thought I could play,
but Mum came outside and she took it away!

I really miss my giant pot of sticky, gooey slime.

Dragon Wishes

If dragons were wishes, then mine would come true.
I'd wish for a dragon, yes, that's what I'd do.
I'd wish…. for a journey, past glistening stars.
Away from these houses and roads full of cars.

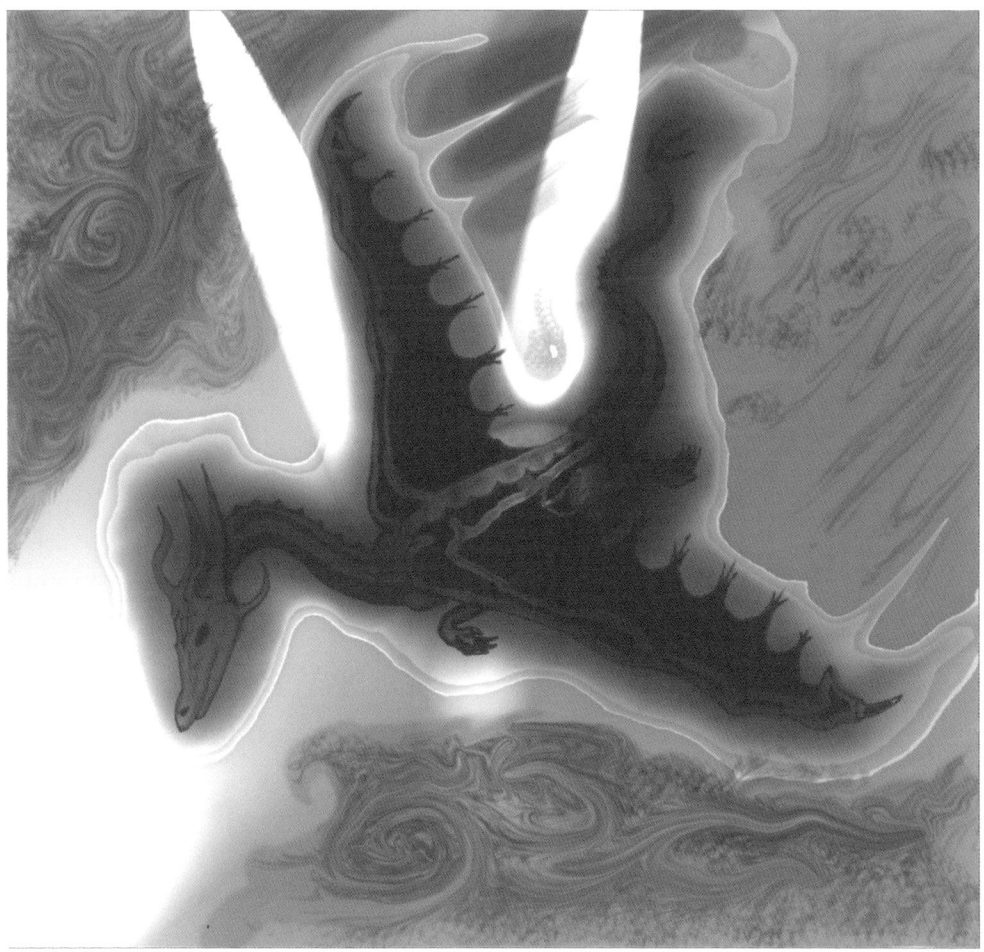

I'd wish….. to fly on dragon wings, holding on so tight;
gliding over rooftops, in the middle of the night.
I'd wish…..to rest on dragon wings, with moonlight everywhere,
sliding down each moonbeam, with stardust in my hair.

Dragons Were Here

People in Asia and Europe too,
tell us amazing things their dragons could do

and...

all over the world there are legends and tales,
of these awesome creatures with their claws and their scales.

Some living in water, some living in caves,
controlling the weather, the land and the waves.

Bringing good luck to those who were strong;
to those who were kind and never did wrong....

Some breathing fire, destroying the land,
swooping and sweeping over hills, sea and sand.

Flapping and gliding - big wings open wide,
setting fire to the forests - so nowhere to hide.

Yes....
all over the world there are legends or tales
of these awesome creatures with their claws and their scales.

Wow they look scary, but beautiful too.
If you could meet one, just what would you do?

Awesome Storm

Wind is wailing wildly.
Land is drenched in rain.
Sploshing rain from rooftop,
is gushing down the drain.
I see the jagged lightning,
fearsome, blue and bright
and hear the thunder crashing
in the middle of the night.

Tiles are rattling on the roof.
I'm sure the house just shook.
I tiptoe to my window,
to take a closer look.
The night looks 'just amazing'...
the black sky streaked with light.
A thunder storm is awesome,
In the middle of the night!

Did you know? The air around lightning is five times hotter than the surface of the sun.

Mum's Car Alarm Won't Stop its Whine....

Mum's car alarm won't stop its whine.
I'd switch it off if it were mine.
With a beep and a bleep and a siren sound
It's meant to warn us when someone's around,
but.....
It shrieks and wails when it starts to rain. **Listen**.....
There it goes.... oh not again!
What a horrid sound. It gave me a scare.
What does it mean? Is someone there?
Is there a person, a cat or a dog?
Is there a mouse, a rat or a frog?
NO.....
Mum's car alarm just hates the rain. **Listen**.....
There it goes.... **oh not again!**

19

Verity the Venomous Viper

Look out!
It's Verity the venomous viper,
going absolutely hyper.

    Escaped from her glass vivarium.
    Heading past the fish aquarium
    and through the herb – herbarium.

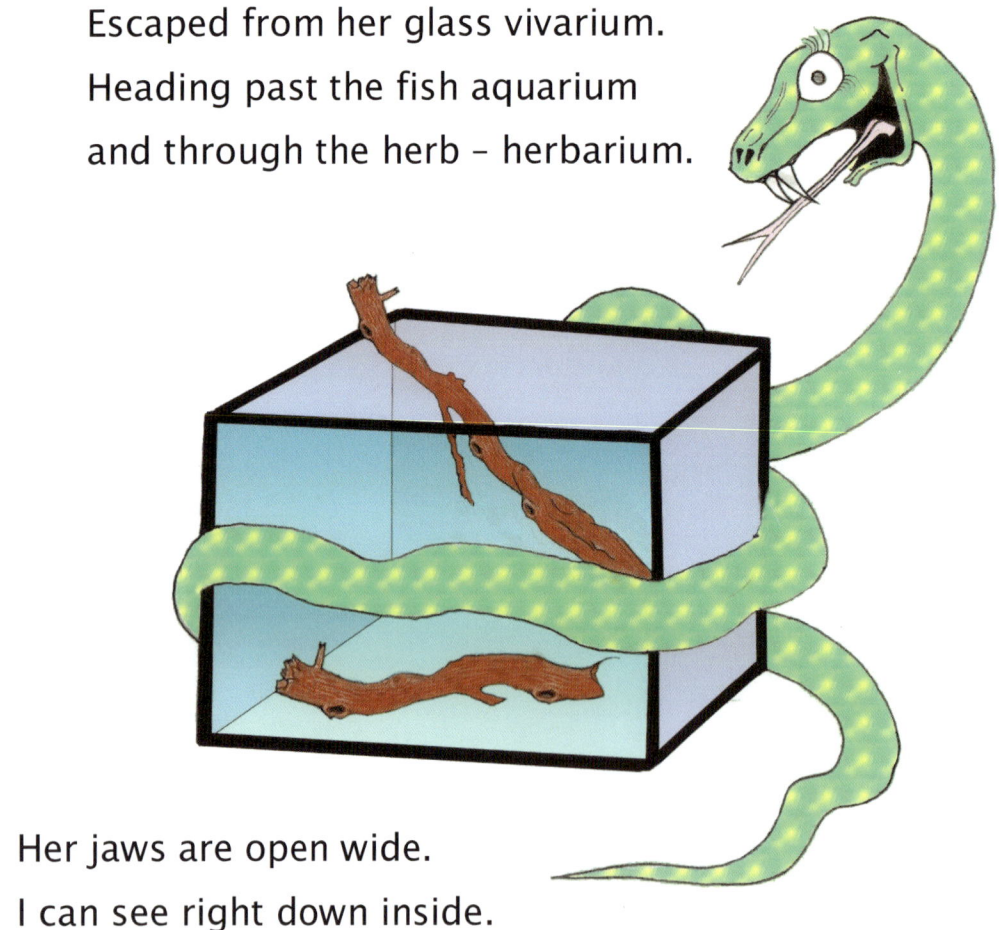

Her jaws are open wide.
I can see right down inside.

    Fangs forward for attack.
    You'll make a tasty snack.

Let me help you quick!

I'll distract her with a stick.

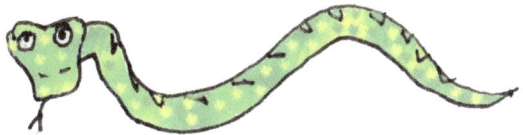

Cool!

Excellent! She's locked in safe and sound.

Now just her friend Vincent to be found!

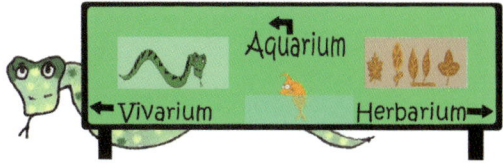

Did you know? When a viper closes his/her mouth, the scary, extra-long fangs fold flat against the roof of the mouth. If the fangs didn't fold flat, vipers would bite themselves!

21

Itchy, Twitchy Fleas

Itchy, twitchy fleas.
I'm scratching at my knees.
It's like a strange disease
and nothing will appease.

So....

Please, please, please,
protect your pets from fleas,
unless you want all these,
scratching at your knees.

Did you know? William Blake, the famous poet and artist, painted a picture called 'The Ghost of a Flea'.

Uncle's New Beard

It's ferocious, it's atrocious.
It gave the cat a fright.
It's all hairy. It's all scary.
It really looks a sight.

It's all weird. It's your beard.
It's grizzly, green and bright.
It's a change. It's real strange,
since you dyed it green last night.

Soggy Socks

My dog likes to chew socks,
especially when they're mine.
She sees them there, ready to wear,
then gives a little whine....

She takes them away, off to play,
until she needs to eat.
Then runs to me, wags her tail
and drops them at my feet.

So....

I'm left with a pair of soggy socks,
each day, to wear to school.
They're covered in fur, smelly too
and I think they're really cool!

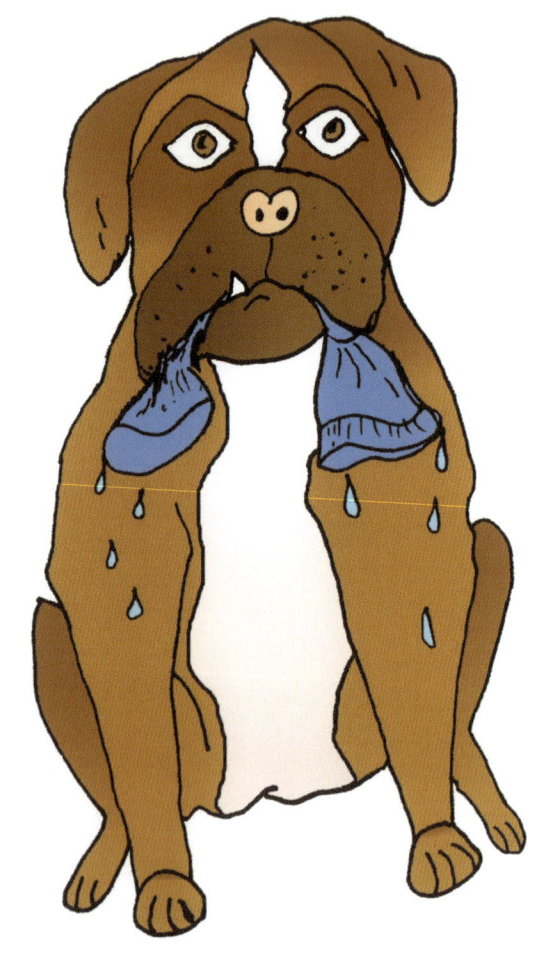

> **Did you know?** Dogs use their amazing sense of smell to help them to learn about their world. They are always sniffing around! Dogs also have excellent hearing. They can hear some 'far away' and 'high pitch' sounds that humans cannot hear at all.

Text!   My big sister is always texting.....

She texts in the morning, at noon and at night.
Her school work is a mess, but.....her text is always right.
She talks in text. She walks in text, well.....
she would if she knew how.
If I just go and find her.....

she'll be texting right now!

Big Brother's Chewing Gum Surprise

My brother is always chewing gum. He leaves it everywhere.
He chews it up, then takes it out. It really isn't fair....
There's chewing gum in the kitchen, chewing gum in the hall
and chewing gum in the living room. It's stuck on every wall.
There's chewing gum on the radiator, all sticky in the heat
and chewing gum on the toilet - yes...stuck right on the seat!
One day I'm going to cast a spell and turn his gum to glue.
It will stick his tongue and lips and teeth

and..... he won't be able to chew!

Did you know? People have been chewing gum for thousands of years. The Ancient Greeks chewed gum made from tree resin.

There's a Lazy Lizard in my Bedroom – Lying on my Bed!

There's a lazy lizard in my bedroom,
lying on my bed.
I'm supposed to be there sleeping,
but the lizard's there instead.

She should be in the garden,
resting by a tree;
not relaxing, in my bedroom,
just staring up at me.

There's a lazy lizard in my bedroom,
lying on my bed.
Perhaps I'll go in the garden
and sleep out there instead!

Did you know? If caught by a predator most lizards will wriggle away, leaving their tails behind. Later.....each lizard will grow a new tail.

Parents, carers and teachers….
you may... like to use some of these ideas for discussion and discovery

Please simplify or extend these ideas, to meet the needs and interests of your children. You may need to support each child's understanding re: some word meanings (for example: 'unique', 'herbarium', 'legend' or 'appease'). Think carefully about the type of questions you will ask each child.

Closed-ended questions tend to involve each child in a simple 'yes/no' type answer; **for example:** "<u>What colour</u> was uncle's new beard?" will probably receive a short factual, one-word answer 'green' (see poem p23). It **is** a useful question and valuable in prompting a vocal response, particularly from younger/less vocal children, but **to truly make the most of discussion opportunities it is helpful to include a good selection of open-ended questions.**

Open ended questions can inspire a more varied and thoughtful response and generally do 'not' require a specific 'right' or 'wrong' answer. For example: "<u>Why</u> do you think uncle dyed his beard green?" may prompt a range of ideas and answers, **drawing on the imagination, curiosity, vocabulary, reasoning skills, knowledge and experience of each child.**

Ultimately, open-ended questions can help children and adults to enjoy a unique and valuable experience, whilst strengthening positive relationships and building confidence and respect.

Here are some sample questions to ask children and some ideas for further research, discovery and discussion together, using books/internet. I hope you have fun!

If I had a Dragon (Page 5)
- ◊ I wonder what other annoying or funny things a dragon might do…
- ◊ If you could have any strange pet what would you choose? Why?

The School Inspector and the Giant African Millipede (Pages 6 - 7)
- ◊ The school inspector gave *"…a long, cold stare"* - what could this mean?

Discover more about Giant African Millipedes. For example: natural habitat, food, lifestyle and main predators.

Back to School Tomorrow (Pages 8 - 9)

◊ The child in the poem feels *"...a cool excitement and a tiny bit of fear"* what could make you feel like this? Why?

◊ What can we do when we feel worried about something?

◊ Why is it good to meet new people and see new places?

Opportunity to link with the child's personal, social and emotional well-being – encouraging positivity and confidence in each new experience.

Hooray for Ginger Hair and Freckles (Page 10)

◊ How did this poem make you feel? Why?

◊ What makes you unique?

◊ What can you do if someone is bullying you?

Opportunity to focus on personal, social and emotional well-being. Encourage your children to be proud of their individual looks, characteristics and skills. If you are a teacher – consider contacting relevant anti-bullying organisations. Have some leaflets available for children to take home.

I See a Bright, Bright Star (Page 11)

◊ I wonder how many different types of stars there are...

Use a telescope, books or a computer to discover more about astronomy.

Our Grandma Lives on a Star (Page 11)

◊ How does this poem make you feel? Why?

Consider strong links to the child's emotional well-being – ensure you **listen with respect and empathy to any shared experiences.** Some children may question the use of the word heaven - encourage respect for all views. If you are a teacher, consider contacting relevant bereavement support organisations for children and families. Have some leaflets available for children to take home.

Slime Crime (Pages 12 - 14)

◊ What would 'you' do with a giant pot of green slime?

◊ What is the messiest, worst mistake you have ever made?

Opportunity for some simple science....discover various safe ways of making slime.

Dragon Wishes (Page 15)

◊   How might it feel to slide down a moonbeam?

◊   If you could go on an exciting journey – where would you go and why?

Opportunity to link with simple astronomy, the cosmos or perhaps space travel….

Dragons Were Here (Pages 16 - 17)

◊   If you could meet a dragon, what would you do?

◊   I wonder if dragons really existed…

◊   Some dragons were said to breath fire. I wonder how they could do this…

Discover dragon legends together – link to various parts of the world and discover the various landscapes and cultures connected with each legend. Link with festivals, involving dragons, such as Chinese New Year.

Awesome Storm (Page 18)

◊   How do you feel when you hear thunder and see lightning?

◊   I wonder how many types of lightning there are…

◊   I wonder what causes thunder…

Opportunity to inspire curiosity and to promote understanding of dramatic weather.

Mum's Car Alarm Won't Stop its Whine (Page 19)

◊   I wonder why the alarm 'didn't like rain'…

◊   Tell me about any sounds you hate…

Discover more about alarms and how they work (for example: burglar or fire alarms).

Verity the Venomous Viper (Page 20 - 21)

◊   What might happen next?

◊   Can you think of any other creatures you could keep in a vivarium?

Discover more about various types of vipers: the many parts of the world they inhabit, their prey and their main predators.

Itchy, Twitchy Fleas (Page 22)

◊ I wonder what makes a flea jump really high…

◊ How can we make sure fleas don't live on our pets?

Opportunity to discover the names and characteristics of parasites found on or in animals or humans.

Uncle's New Beard (Page 23)

◊ Why do you think uncle dyed his beard green?

Discuss the need to look and feel unique. Or: link to the various things people might do to raise money for charities – <u>dying their beards</u>, shaving their hair, baking cakes, long walks, parachute jumps…

Soggy Socks (Page 24)

◊ Why do you think the dog liked to chew socks?

Discover some interesting animal facts: Why do some mammals have wet noses? 'How' and 'why' do cats purr? 'Why' is a dog's sense of smell so amazing?

Text (Page 25)

◊ Are smartphones good or bad? Why?

Discover how we lived 'years ago' before modern technology.

Big Brother's Chewing Gum Surprise (Page 25)

◊ What is the most annoying thing that someone you know does?

◊ I wonder if gum can be recycled…

Link with topics involving the environment…keeping streets free from gum, cans and other rubbish. Discuss the value of recycling. Encourage respect for our towns, cities and countryside.

There's a Lazy Lizard in my Bedroom - Lying on my Bed (Pages 26 - 27)

◊ I wonder how the lizard found her way into the house and onto the bed…

◊ Do you think the lizard will still be there in the morning? Why?

◊ What could happen next?

Discover the different types of lizards and the various areas of the world they inhabit; plus, their prey and their predators.

The author.....

A. F. B. Griffey has a BA in Early Childhood Studies and enjoyed many happy years teaching and presenting creative activities in pre-schools and schools. She has lectured in colleges, within Early Years Education and Health & Social Care departments. Her poems have been tested and acclaimed by primary school and pre-school children and her first book *Revenge of the Goldfish* was published by *Louannvee* in 2016. She has three grown up boys, a grandchild, a lively Labrador dog called Canada and a cute cat called Tchaikovsky. A. F. B. Griffey lives in the UK and adores adventure, travel, running on the beach with her dog, music, poetry and writing.

The Illustrator.....

R. W. B. is happiest whilst travelling to far away lands, filled with interesting scenery and exciting places to explore. He would like to live somewhere, where the sun is always shining! He spends much time observing, photographing and sketching mini-beasts, reptiles and other small creatures; often turning his sketches into humorous cartoons. His skills have been used to design logos and business leaflets and in 2016 he provided the illustrations for A. F. B. Griffey's *Revenge of the Goldfish*.

Printed in Great Britain
by Amazon